My First Bookkeeping System

How to do Bookkeeping & Financial Reporting
using a spreadsheet,
only a spreadsheet, and
nothing but a spreadsheet

Martin Mosfeldt, MBA

Copyright © 2014 Martin Mosfeldt

All rights reserved.

ISBN: 1502519674

ISBN-13: 978-1502519672

CONTENTS

1	Introduction	1
2	Bookkeeping	5
3	Profit & Loss	9
4	Balance Sheet	11
5	Cash Flow	13
6	Explanatory Notes	15
7	Groups of Companies	19
8	Journal & Ledger	23
9	Errors	25
10	Exercises	29
11	Troubleshooting	33
12	Quick Reference	37
	Index	39

1 INTRODUCTION

Background

Louie hadn't got the tablet he wanted for a birthday present. With the bills piling up, uncle Donald was not likely to fix this, anytime soon.

Louie had an idea that he could use the tablet to make enough money to pay for it, but the idea bit its own tail. To buy the tablet he needed money, and to get the money, he needed the tablet.

Huey, Dewey and Louie had each gotten $200 cash for presents. Between them, the brothers had $600, enough to buy a $499 tablet, but Huey wanted a bicycle to bring out newspapers with, and Dewey wanted to save his money for later.

Louie got on the phone to his granduncle Scrooge. It took Louie a while to talk his way past receptionists and secretaries, but eventually he had Scrooge McDuck on the line.

"What do you mean, you need money?" uncle Scrooge asked, and without waiting for an answer, he continued: "Everybody needs money, money doesn't grow on trees, do you think I made the few pennies I own by giving money away?"

Louie explained that he needed a bookkeeping machine, a tablet to do bookkeeping on. Bookkeeping, Louie knew, was a one of his uncle's interests.

"Hmmm. So you want to do bookkeeping. Hmmm." Uncle Scrooge was wavering, but curiosity got the better of him, and he asked: "Suppose you got your machine, and I'm not saying you will have it, how would you pay for it?"

Louie explained that he would open a lawn sale of fresh fruit, using fruit he would gather from gardens in the neighborhood. "They will let me have the fruit if I pick it, so it doesn't lie on their lawns and rot."

"Tell you what, son," uncle Scrooge said, "I'm feeling unusually generous today. If you promise not to tell anyone, I'll give you $100 when you've shown that you can run the business and work the machine."

Louie hurried to say thank you and end the conversation, before uncle Scrooge changed his mind. He hung up and called grandma Duck.

"Of course I can keep a secret," grandma Duck said, "and if uncle Scrooge really pays the $100, I'll top them with another $100. But, mind you, getting him to open his wallet will not be easy."

In spite of the promised gifts, Louis' finances still had a chicken- and egg problem, because he needed the tablet to get the gifts, but he needed the gifts to afford the tablet, which brings us to Huey's and Dewey's $200.

"Sure, you can borrow our $200 until we need them ourselves", Huey and Dewey answered, when Louie asked for a loan. "Just keep them out of uncle Donald's reach. If you lose them, you still owe us." They gave Louie four one hundred dollar bills. Louie put the bills in his pocket and made a mental note to buy a $25 moneybox with a lock.

The next morning Louis' lawn sale opened with two large boxes of apples, a tablet, a money-box, and a pile of paper bags he'd gotten for free. By noon he had sold twenty-four three-dollar bags, but then Huey stopped by and wanted his money back, because he'd found a very nice bicycle advertised at $185.

"I've only got $148," Louie said, counting what was in his moneybox and giving it to Huey, "but I'll make the rest tomorrow". Next morning Louis' lawn sale opened for business, but business was not as good as the day before, and when Huey stopped by to collect the remaining $52, there was only $39 in the moneybox. Even though he had not been paid back in full, Huey was happy with the $39, because he now had $187, which covered the bicycle.

Louie sat waiting outside uncle Scrooge's office with his tablet, to collect the promised one hundred dollars. On learning his errand, the secretary warned Louie that he might be in for a long wait, because uncle Scrooge was not easy to get to part with his money.

Louie was nobody's fool. He knew his uncle and snuck around to the back door, where he caught him, shortly after.

"Ah, there you are my boy," uncle Scrooge said, "I'm on my way to a meeting, but have my secretary find a time where I'm available, and then we can discuss the matter of my one-hundred dollars."

"No reason to arrange a meeting," Louie said, "here's my tablet. As you can see, it shows that I can run my business. Can I have my one-hundred dollars, please?"

MY FIRST BOOKKEPING SYSTEM

Getting Started

So what did Louie show uncle Scrooge on the tablet? The short answer is, "a financial report". In this little book we shall make that financial report, using double-entry bookkeeping and a spreadsheet program called Google Sheets, which is free on the open Internet. There is another spreadsheet program one can also use, which is called Excel, but it costs something.

Google Sheets works well with Google's own browser, Chrome. Using whatever browser you have, Google the term "chrome". Google will find a page where you can download Chrome. Once you got Chrome, make it your default browser.

Google the term: "sheets". Again, Google will find a page for you, where you can download the Sheets program. If you want, you can install Google Drive, too – I did, and I think it's nice.

If you prefer using Excel, it comes as a program package from Microsoft, usually together with Microsoft Office. I won't go through how to install it, but it is fully as good as Sheets, and more widely used in commercial businesses.

Either way, when you start your spreadsheet program the first time, Sheets or Excel, you should see something like this:

	A	B	C	D	E	F	G	H	I
1									
2									
3									
4									
5									
6									
7									

This table of 'cells', as they are called, can be made to do just about anything a computer program can do. In this book, we will use it to make a double-entry bookkeeping system.

Design

Our bookkeeping system will use six columns in the spreadsheet, namely the columns A, B, C, D, E and F. In the top, say the first 20 or 25 rows, will be the financial reports. Below, in the remaining rows, will be the bookkeeping records, one or maybe two for each time money or goods changes hands.

Having the whole system in one sheet is smart, because it is simple. It is very easy to make spreadsheets systems complicated; the trick is to make them simple.

Reference Model

To see how the system works, have a look at this illustration.

In the top are financial reports. Each one has a title, some report lines, and a sum. There are four financial reports that one normally finds in a bookkeeping system, namely:

- Profit & Loss
- Assets
- Liabilities & Equity
- Cash flow

Title
    Report line
    Report line
Sum

Title
    Report line
    Report line
Sum
-
-
-

Bookkeeping record
Bookkeeping record
Bookkeeping record
Bookkeeping record
Bookkeeping record
Bookkeeping record
-
-
-

Below the financial reports are bookkeeping records, which are generated by the business, and which are used to calculate report lines.

One does not have to calculate the report lines oneself, because the spreadsheet does that automatically.

The arrow is meant to illustrate that the spreadsheet program does calculations on bookkeeping records and puts results into report lines.

There can be lots of bookkeeping records, or there can be a few; that depends on the business. To keep things simple, it is usually a good idea to avoid having too many bookkeeping records, say, no more than a few hundred.

2 BOOKKEEPING

	C	D
30	Huey	200.00
31	Dewey	200.00
32	Tablet	-499.00
33	Money-box	-25.00
34	Apples	3.00
35	Apples	9.00
36	Apples	18.00
37	Apples	21.00
38	Apples	21.00
39	Huey	-148.00
40	Apples	39.00
41	Huey	-39.00

The bookkeeping records for Louis' business start out looking like this. In cells C30 and D30 is the $200 Louie borrowed from Huey, and in cells C31 and D31 is the $200 he borrowed from Dewey. Then he bought the tablet and the moneybox, sold many apples, and paid Huey back in part.

Why don't you make a spreadsheet of your own, with Louie's or your own bookkeeping? That will make this book more fun, because you try things instead of just reading about them.

Notice how Louie, when he sold his first bag of apples, recorded $3, but then later stopped recording each time he sold a bag, and instead recorded first three, then six, and then seven at a time. This is how one keeps the number of records down. In a lot of small shops, the money in the cash register at the end of the day is the only thing that is recorded, instead of recording each time a sale is made.

Huey got a receipt when he bought his tablet and his moneybox. When you run a business, you keep your receipts in your moneybox or in a separate binder, and write a number on each one. In the bookkeeping, you record what date is on the receipt, and what number it has, so that you can find the receipt to prove that the asset in question is really yours, and that you have a warranty claim on the merchant that sold it to you, if something is the matter.

	A	B	C	D
30		October 10	Huey	200.00
31		October 10	Dewey	200.00
32	1	October 10	Tablet	-499.00
33	2	October 10	Money-box	-25.00
34		October 11	Apples	3.00
35		October 11	Apples	9.00
36		October 11	Apples	18.00
37		October 11	Apples	21.00
38		October 11	Apples	21.00
39		October 11	Huey	-148.00
40		October 11	Apples	39.00
41		October 12	Huey	-39.00

Huey gave the receipts for his tablet and his moneybox numbers one and two, as you can see in cell A32 and A33. In the cells B32 and B33 you can see, that the purchases were both made on the tenth of October.

Huey is using a month-date format for recording, but the spreadsheet program has many other formats one can use. For example, a common American format would be 1/10/2014, and a common European format would be 10-1-2014. Also, Huey is using a period for the decimal separator between the dollars and the cents, which is common in America and England. In most of Europe a comma is used, so for example the loan from Dewey would read 200,00 instead of 200.00.

Accounting

The bookkeeping work consists of assigning two accounts to each bookkeeping record, as shown here:

	A	B	C	D	E	F
30		October 10	Huey	200.00	60 Huey	40 Cash
31		October 10	Dewey	200.00	61 Dewey	40 Cash
32	1	October 10	Tablet	-499.00	30 Equipment	40 Cash
33	2	October 10	Money-box	-25.00	20 Expenses	40 Cash
34		October 11	Apples	3.00	10 Revenues	40 Cash
35		October 11	Apples	9.00	10 Revenues	40 Cash
36		October 11	Apples	18.00	10 Revenues	40 Cash
37		October 11	Apples	21.00	10 Revenues	40 Cash
38		October 11	Apples	21.00	10 Revenues	40 Cash
39		October 11	Huey	-148.00	60 Huey	40 Cash
40		October 11	Apples	39.00	10 Revenues	40 Cash
41		October 12	Huey	-39.00	60 Huey	40 Cash

MY FIRST BOOKKEPING SYSTEM

Because there are two accounts assigned to each record, it is called a 'double-entry' bookkeeping system; if it were 'single-entry', there would only be one account assigned to each record.

What the accounts mean is best explained with examples. In row 30, for example, E30 says that the $200 are owed to Huey, and F30 says that they were received in the form of cash. In row 34, the sale of apples generated revenue equal to $3 cash. In row 33, the purchase of a moneybox generated expenses of $25 cash.

As of now, Louie's is a cash-only business; so all payments are received or delivered in the form of cash. Later, we shall see non-cash payments, too.

The accounts have numbers, 10 for 'Revenue', 20 for 'Expenses', and so on. They don't have to have numbers for the system to work, but in practice they always do, so one doesn't have to worry about getting accounts confused.

Retained Earnings

Louie's own account in his own business is called 'Equity'. What his business earns is retained as equity until he withdraws it. 'Withdrawal' is when Louie takes cash from his moneybox to use for himself. Withdrawals are charged to Louie's equity account and do not affect his business' earnings.

	A	B	C	D	E	F
29			Automatic	86.00	50 Equity	

A special bookkeeping record, which sits before all the other records in row 29, maintains the equity account automatically. This bookkeeping record has only one account instead of the normal two, and it doesn't have a date, either.

The number in cell D29 is computed automatically with a formula that looks like this:

$$=D4$$

Instead of entering 86.00 in cell D29, you enter =D4, and the 86.00 is computed automatically. Why this works, we shall see in the next chapter.

3 PROFIT & LOSS

	A	B	C
1	**Profit & Loss**		
2		10 Revenues	111
3		20 Expenses	-25
4	**Net income**		86

Louie's income statement, his P&L, has two report lines: Revenue and Expenses. The =C4 mentioned in the previous chapter takes the number in cell C4 and copies it to cell D29, automatically. In this way the profit the business earns is automatically retained on the equity account. The cell C2 is computed automatically using a formula that looks like this:

```
=SUMIFS(D:D,E:E,B2)-SUMIFS(D:D,F:F,B2)
```

If your country is one of those that use comma instead of period for decimal separator, it will instead look like this:

```
=SUMIFS(D:D;E:E;B2)-SUMIFS(D:D;F:F;B2)
```

This formula browses through all the bookkeeping records and sums up the ones that are charged to the account: 10 Revenues, which it finds in cell B2. That will be all the rows in the spreadsheet with apples, that is, rows 33, 34, 35, 36, 37 and 39. If you add up the numbers in those rows, you will see that Louie has in fact sold $111 worth of apples, so far.

If you copy/paste the SUMIFS formula from cell C2 to cell C3, the spreadsheet program will automatically change the row number in the formula so it reads:

```
=SUMIFS(D:D,E:E,B3)-SUMIFS(D:D,F:F,B3)
```

Since the formula in cell C3 now finds another account in B3, namely: 20 Expenses, it finds row 32 with the moneybox, and puts that number in cell C3. The formulas are coded using matrix array notation, as in $D:$D. This means all the records are summed up, no matter how many there are. The cell C4 is computed using the formula:

```
=SUM(C2:C3)
```

Since there are only two report lines that need to be summed up, one could also have written

```
=C2+C3
```

However, the SUM function is smarter, because it also works when there are more than two report lines.

Accounts

The texts in the report lines in column B are also the names of accounts that one can put in bookkeeping records. To make sure that misspelled or missing accounts do not find their way into the bookkeeping, the system is set up with data validation. If you click on 'Data' and 'Validation' in your spreadsheet program, you can enter this:

Data validation

Cell range	E:F	
Criteria	List from range ◆	B1:B26

This makes an automatic drop-down list in each of the cells in the bookkeeping records where account names are supposed to go. In this way, one only has to type the account names once, to select them from a drop-down list the rest of the time. If one ticks off 'Reject input', the spreadsheet program will automatically protect against misspelled account names in bookkeeping records. At the time of writing, data validation didn't work on smartphones, but it didn't cause any trouble, either; it just wasn't there.

4 BALANCE SHEET

	A	B	C	D
6	Assets			Primo
7		30 Equipment	499	0
8		40 Cash	0	200
9		41 Bank	0	0
10	Total assets		499	200
11				
12	Liabilities & Equity			Primo
13		50 Equity	286	200
14		60 Huey	13	0
15		61 Dewey	200	0
16	Total liabilities		499	200

This is Louie's balance sheet. Primo means the start of the year.

Row 7 says he didn't have any equipment at the start of the year, but now he has $499's worth.

Row 8 says he had $200 cash at the start of the year, but now they're gone.

Row 10 shows that his total assets amounted to $200 at the start of the year, and that they have now grown to $499. Row 13 says that his equity has grown from $200 at the start of the year, to $286, now. Rows 14 and 15 says that he owes Huey $13 and Dewey $200.

The formula for the assets in row 7 is

```
=D7-SUMIFS(D:D,E:E,B7)+SUMIFS(D:D,F:F,B7)
```

The formula for the liabilities & equity in row 13 is

```
=D13+SUMIFS(D:D,E:E,B13)-SUMIFS(D:D,F:F,B13)
```

If you copy/paste the formula in row 7 to row 8 and row 9, the spreadsheet program automatically adjusts the row number in the formula, and likewise when you copy/paste the formula in row 13 to row 14 and row 15.

Notice that total liabilities and total assets are the same. This is no coincidence. On the contrary, it is the whole point of doing double entry bookkeeping instead of single entry, because it automatically reveals if there are errors.

The job of correcting errors in the bookkeeping until assets and liabilities match is called: "balancing the books". It's called 'books' in plural even though there is only one sheet, because formerly the ledger would span numerous volumes; at least one per fiscal year, and often several.

To check that the books balance, one can use conditional formatting. Select the whole sheet by clicking on the upper, left corner of the sheet, the cell to the left of 'A' and above '1'. If you click 'Format' and 'Conditional formatting', you should see something like this:

Conditional formatting

Text contains ◆		Format:		Text color:		Range:	
				Background color:			

Fill out the fields with 'Is not equal to' =C16 for the range C10:D10. Add another rule, and fill out its fields with 'Is not equal to' =C10 for the range C16:D16. In both rules, for text color, select bright red. See how it works by entering an incorrect number in cell D7; you should see total assets and liabilities turn bright, alarming red, because the books no longer balance.

5 CASH FLOW

	A	B	C
18	**Cash flow**		
19	**Earnings**		86
20		30 Equipment	-499
21	**Cash flow from operations**		-413
22		60 Huey	13
23		61 Dewey	200
24		41 Bank	0
25	**Cash flow from finance**		213
26	**Net cash flow**		-200

This is Louie's cash flow. As you can see, Louie's business has been profitable but cash-flow negative, which is typical for start-ups.

The report lines in the cash flow say where cash came from, and where it went. Even though Louie has made $86 selling apples, the negative cash flow from his equipment purchase has taken $200 out of his available cash reserves, and put him in debt $213 to Huey and Dewey.

Cash flows are always ordered like this, with the earnings on top, because they are used to answer questions like: "If we made $86, where's the cash?" The accounts in the cash flow are sorted with operational accounts first and financial accounts later, and with a sum for each. The sums are called 'cash flow from operations' and 'cash flow from finance', and the sum of the sums is called 'Net cash flow'.

The formula for a report line in a cash flow row, say, row 20 is:

```
=SUMIFS(D:D,E:E,B20)-SUMIFS(D:D,F:F,B20)
```

This is the same formula that was used for the report lines in the profit & loss. The difference is, that in the cash flow, the accounts are the ones from the balance sheet. Therefore, another way to explain the cash flow, is to say: "It is the formula for profit & loss, but applied to the accounts from the balance sheet".

One can use this for data validation on the cells B20, B22, B23 and B24. If you select cells B22:B24 and click 'Data' and 'Validation', you can specify

Data validation

Cell range   B22:B24

Criteria   List from range ◆ B7:B15

This makes an automatic drop-down list in the cells in the cash flow where account names are supposed to go. As said before, at the time of writing, this didn't work on smartphones, but it didn't cause any trouble, either.

In row 19 and row 28 could have been the equity and the cash accounts from the balance sheet, account numbers 40 and 50, but instead those lines are written like it is usually done in a cash flow report. Therefore cell C19 must be =C4, and cell C28 must be =C21+C25.

Notice that C26 balances D8-D7. To check this, set up conditional formatting that colors C26 red when the cash flow doesn't balance:

Conditional formatting

Is not equal to ◆ =D8-D7   Format: ✔ Text color: ✔   Range:
                                      Background color: ☐   C26

6 EXPLANATORY NOTES

Near the back door to the Scrooge McDuck building, looking at Louie's tablet, granduncle Scrooge saw Louie's financial report and bookkeeping, which is shown on the next two pages. It took him two seconds flat to understand what that meant, namely that Louie knew what he was doing, and that $100 thus were about to exit the hard-to-open McDuck wallet.

"Congratulations. I see you've been doing well, but have no money in the bank." Uncle Scrooge had already figured out what to do to keep his wallet shut. "Let me have my treasurer transfer $100 to you bank. What is your account number, young man?"

Louie explained that he didn't have a bank account. "I see," Uncle Scrooge said, "let me help you with that. It so happens that I own the McDuck bank. Go there the day after tomorrow, and you'll find an account to your name, with a $100 deposit." Louie thanked his uncle and hurried out before something happened that would change things.

Louie entered a bookkeeping record to show that he now had $100 in the bank, and went back to selling apples. His supply of apples was waning, because the best ones he'd already collected, and those remaining were not as good. By end-of-day he had $21 in his moneybox.

Checking on his finances, Louie saw that his revenues now amounted to $232. To keep track of how much revenue was from apples and how much was from other sources, he added a note to the end of his sheet, below the bookkeeping records. This note, he figured, was for his own use, and by putting it way down at the end of the sheet, he could show his report to others without showing the note.

MARTIN MOSFELDT

	A	B	C	D	E	F
1	Profit & Loss		YTD			
2		10 Revenues	232			
3		20 Expenses	-25			
4	Net income		207			
5						
6	Assets		YTD	Primo		
7		30 Equipment	499	0		
8		40 Cash	21	200		
9		41 Bank	100	0		
10	Total assets		620	200		
11						
12	Liabilities		YTD	Primo		
13		50 Equity	407	200		
14		60 Huey	13	0		
15		61 Dewey	200	0		
16	Total liabilities		620	200		
17						
18	Cash flow		YTD			
19	Earnings		207			
20		30 Equipment	-499			
21	Cash flow operations		-292			
22		60 Huey	13			
23		61 Dewey	200			
24		41 Bank	-100			
25	Cash flow f. finance		113			
26	Net cash flow		-179			
27						
28		Date	Text	Amount		
29			Automatic	86.00	50 Equity	
30		October 10	Huey	200.00	60 Huey	40 Cash
31		October 10	Dewey	200.00	61 Dewey	40 Cash
32	1	October 10	Tablet	-499.00	30 Equipment	40 Cash
33	2	October 10	Money-box	-25.00	20 Expenses	40 Cash
34		October 11	Apples	3.00	10 Revenues	40 Cash

MY FIRST BOOKKEPING SYSTEM

	A	B	C	D	E	F
35		October 11	Apples	9.00	10 Revenues	40 Cash
36		October 11	Apples	18.00	10 Revenues	40 Cash
37		October 11	Apples	21.00	10 Revenues	40 Cash
38		October 11	Apples	21.00	10 Revenues	40 Cash
39		October 11	Huey	-148.00	60 Huey	40 Cash
40		October 11	Apples	39.00	10 Revenues	40 Cash
41		October 12	Huey	-39.00	60 Huey	40 Cash
42		October 13	Bonus	100.00	10 Revenues	41 Bank
43		October 13	Apples	21.00	10 Revenues	40 Cash
44						
45						
46						
47	**Note**					
48		GUS	100.00			
49		GMD				
50		Apples	132.00			
51	**Revenue**		232.00			

To keep his granduncle Scrooge's rare generosity secret, Louie's note used abbreviations, instead of writing in plain text where the money came from. Also Louie figured there was no reason to put grandma Duck in a position where she had to explain why she had said *yes* to Louie and *no* to someone else, especially since her $100 was not realized, yet.

Formulas in notes are flexible. Notes have many uses, and each use takes its own formula. In the case of Louie's revenue note, the report lines GUS and GMD are literal numbers. The formula for the revenue in cell C51 is

$$=C2$$

The formula for the 'Apples' line in cell C50 is

$$=C51-C48-C49$$

7 GROUPS OF COMPANIES

Huey, Dewey and Louie were in conference. Dewey was concerned for his $200 that he had loaned to Louie.

"If there aren't any more apples this year, how are you going to pay me back, anytime soon?" Dewey asked. Louie explained that he had an account with the McDuck bank, which held $100, and which would soon grow to $200. Dewey had a look at Louie's financial report, and this reassured him so much that he asked:

"Why don't you keep my $200 in your bank account until I need them? I don't have a bank account, my money is safer with you. Where did you get all this money?"

"Basically, from apples," Louie answered, dodging the last question, "and I'll be happy to keep your $200 for you for as long as you like, and go collect them from the bank when you want them back." He asked Huey how the newspaper deliveries were doing.

"I have no idea," Huey answered, "I've brought out 121 papers today, and 143 yesterday, and I'm supposed to get 4 cents per paper, but I haven't been paid yet." They agreed to record Huey's business on Louie's tablet, too.

Adding Another Company

On a PC or a Mac, your spreadsheet can have as many sheets as you like, one for each business' books that you keep. It would be nice if it was like that on all tablets and a smartphones, too, but since the software sometimes won't

	A	B	C	D
1	**Profit & Loss**		YTD	
2		10 Revenues	11	
3		20 Expenses	0	
4	**Net income**		11	
5				
6	**Assets**		YTD	Primo
7		30 Equipment	185	0
8		61 Newspapers	11	0
9		60 Louie	13	0
10		40 Cash	2	200
11	**Total assets**		211	200
12				
13	**Liabilities**		YTD	Primo
14		50 Equity	211	200
15	**Total liabilities**		211	200
16				
17	**Cash flow**		YTD	
18	**Earnings**		11	
19		30 Equipment	-185	
20	**Cash flow from operations**		-174	
21		60 Louie	-13	
22	**Cash flow from finance**		-13	
23	**Net cash flow**		-187	

allow that, in those cases, it is better to make a new spreadsheet for a new business, instead of adding new sheets to an existing one.

Huey's financial reports look the same as Louie's, except the accounts and the numbers differ a little. This is on purpose. It is good to always use the same general way of presenting the facts, because then stakeholders like Scrooge McDuck can grasp the business in a moment.

Notice how the two financial reports, Louie's and Huey's, fit together. In both is recorded that Louie owes Huey $13. In Louie's financial report this is recorded as a liability, and in Huey's it is recorded as an asset.

Notice that where the two businesses overlap, Louie uses the same account numbers and names. This is not always the way it is. You can use any account numbers and names you like, but if they're the same, it is easier to work with and find errors, if something is wrong.

Huey's bookkeeping, which is shown at the top of the next page, has fewer records than Louie's. The money earned for bringing out papers is calculated automatically with the formulas

$$=143*4/100$$

and

$$=121*4/100$$

MY FIRST BOOKKEPING SYSTEM

	A	B	C	D	E	F
25	**Date**		**Text**	**Amount**		
26			Automatic	10.56	50 Equity	
27	October 10		Louie	-200.00	60 Louie	40 Cash
28	October 11		Louie	148.00	60 Louie	40 Cash
29	October 12		Louie	39.00	60 Louie	40 Cash
30	October 12		Bicycle	-185.00	30 Equipment	40 Cash
31	October 12		Papers	4.84	10 Revenues	61 Newspapers
32	October 13		Papers	5.72	10 Revenues	61 Newspapers

Huey uses an account called '61 Newspapers' to record how much he is owed for bringing out papers. When he gets paid in cash, it could be recorded with '61 Newspapers' to the left and '40 Cash' to the right. In principle there is nothing wrong with having an account sometimes to the left and sometimes to the right, but it can get confusing. If you find that confusing, here's what you can do, instead.

When Huey gets paid, say $10.56, make two records, both of them with nothing to the left. The first record puts 10.56 into '40 Cash', and the second record puts -10.56 into '61 Newspapers'. In this way, the books still balance, but no account is allowed to be both left and right. Here's what the recording would look like:

	A	B	C	D	E	F
33		November 1	Payday	10.56		40 Cash
34		November 1	Payday	-10.56		61 Newspapers

8 JOURNAL & LEDGER

A journal is a log of all that happened with the bookkeeping, in date order. If you just remember to put your bookkeeping records in date order when you create them, you automatically have a journal.

Journals are useful if the bookkeeping needs to be moved to another bookkeeping system. Suppose for example that Huey gets his own laptop and wants to take over his own bookkeeping, instead of having Louie do it. If there were no journal, it would be very difficult for Huey to find out what Louie had done with his bookkeeping.

A ledger is like a journal for each single account. A complete ledger would include each account, but with a spreadsheet one does not need a complete ledger. The reason for this is that the spreadsheet program has filtering.

If you select that part of column E which has the bookkeeping records, say from row 29 to 43 in Louie's bookkeeping, and click the funnel symbol, a small funnel will appear in cell E29. If you click that small funnel and clear all the tick marks for all accounts except one, you should see a ledger for that one account. If you click the funnel (not the small one) again, the filtering will stop.

Ledgers are useful to find out if something is wrong with a particular account. If for example Huey couldn't remember how much Louie had paid back on his loan, a filter would show all payments that had been made.

When a plastic card is used to charge payments to a bank account, a filter can be used to show all the payments that should be in the bank account, so one can verify that the bank's bookkeeping agrees with one's own.

Also, most Internet banks have a facility for downloading the movements on a bank account to a spreadsheet, so that one does not have to write everything manually, when doing the bookkeeping.

9 ERRORS

Accounting Practices

The way one does the bookkeeping is called the business' 'accounting practices'. A written summary of the accounting practices is called the 'accounting policy'. Lots of businesses do not have an accounting policy, but there are always accounting practices, even though one might not be aware of them. This is because, as soon as you do bookkeeping, you do it some way, which then becomes your accounting practices.

The bookkeeping is correct if it follows the accounting practices. Therefore, if you do your bookkeeping in some way, you've got to keep doing it that way. If you change your accounting practices, you've got to change them all the way back to the beginning of the bookkeeping.

In the case of Louie, his large investment in a tablet was charged to the '30 Equipment' account, but his small investment in a moneybox was charged to the '20 Expenses' account. Therefore, if Louie some time in the future buys an expensive printer, it should be accounted for like he did with the tablet, because that agrees with his accounting practices. If, sometime in the future, he buys an inexpensive box of alphabetic letters for making outdoor signs, he should charge it to '20 Expenses', just like he did with the moneybox.

In a business that pays taxes and salaries, there are many laws for the accounting practices. In the case of Huey and Louie, it is simpler, but there are still laws. Louie's debt to Huey and Dewey must be correctly accounted for in Louie's books. Recording that the debt has been paid back when it hasn't is called cooking the books, and one is not supposed to do that.

Accounts Organization

Louie uses eight accounts for his bookkeeping:

    10 Revenues

    20 Expenses

    30 Equipment

    40 Cash

    41 Bank

    50 Equity

    60 Huey

    61 Dewey

This is called the 'chart of accounts'. Technically, you can have as many accounts as you like, which you call anything you like. But, if you have many accounts, they should be organized in major and minor accounts, and that takes a more advanced bookkeeping system than the one you are being given here.

The next in line in this series of books explains how to implement a two-level chart of accounts in a spreadsheet system, and a typical commercial bookkeeping package for small businesses will have a two-level chart of accounts, too.

Accounts Naming and Numbering

Since the whole purpose of financial reporting is to present indisputable facts, it is best to name the accounts in a style that doesn't sound funky. If you use funky names for your accounts, readers will infer that your bookkeeping is funky, too, and dispute your reports.

Notice that similar accounts have close numbers. This is generally accepted as the right way to do it. Most businesses have four- or five-digit account numbers, and government account numbers can have twenty!

Accounts List Errors

If you change the name of an account in, say, the balance sheet, you must change its name in the bookkeeping records and the cash flow, too. The data validation will automatically flag cells that need to be changed, provided you remember to tick off 'reject input' when you set it up. As mentioned, at the time of writing, data validation didn't work on smartphones.

Accounting Relations

The total assets must balance the total liabilities. The system automatically checks this, because of the conditional formatting you set up in the chapter about the balance sheet.

The reason the totals must balance is mathematical. All the numbers in the bookkeeping are balanced so they add up to zero.

$$c_1 + c_2 + c_3 \ldots = 0$$

If you split the numbers into three groups called earnings, assets and liabilities, their sum will still be zero.

$$(c_1 + c_2 + c_3 \ldots)_{earnings} + (c_4 + c_5 + c_6 \ldots)_{assets} + (c_7 + c_8 + c_9 \ldots)_{liabilities} = 0$$

Using one number $R = (c_1 + c_2 + c_3 \ldots)_{earnings}$ for retained earnings instead of the earnings group doesn't change the sum either.

$$R + (c_4 + c_5 + c_6 \ldots)_{assets} + (c_7 + c_8 + c_9 \ldots)_{liabilities} = 0$$

Therefore, by moving the assets group to the other side of the equal sign, we have the accounting relation

$$R + (c_7 + c_8 + c_9 \ldots)_{liabilities} = -(c_4 + c_5 + c_6 \ldots)_{assets}$$

If we use one number

$$L = (c_7 + c_8 + c_9 \ldots)_{liabilities}$$

for the liabilities, and another number

$$A = -(c_4 + c_5 + c_6 \ldots)_{assets}$$

for the assets, we can write the accounting relation

$$R + L = A$$

Control Formulas

Remember the way Huey's pay for bringing out newspapers was calculated? This is one of the really smart things about spreadsheets, that you can do a calculation directly by writing an equal sign in the cell, instead of calculating that number with a calculator and entering it manually.

As time goes by, Louie's tablet will lose some of its value, until, one day, it is so old that it won't work anymore. Therefore Louie should record in his books now and then, that his tablet is not worth as much as when he just bought it.

This is called a write-off, and normally one does it at the end of the year. If Louie decides to write off a third of the tablets value, he could calculate the amount to write off directly using

$$=499/3$$

Louie could also decide to write off a third of all his equipment using the formula

$$=C7/3$$

but that wont work, because then the spreadsheet program will try to calculate cell C7 from C7/3, which is a 'circular reference'.

So, which account goes to the left, and which account goes to the right, when you do a write-off? If Louie enters his write-off as a single record, it should look like this:

A	B	C	D	E	F
44	December 31	Write-off	-166.33	20 Expenses	30 Equipment

This can get confusing, because the '30 Equipment' account is to the right instead of to the left, as it normally is. If you agree this is confusing, a better way to record a write-off is with two records, like this:

A	B	C	D	E	F
44	December 31	Write-off	-166.33	20 Expenses	
45	December 31	Write-off	166.33	30 Equipment	

10 EXERCISES

Double-entry bookkeeping is smart, because it automatically detects errors. But what would single be like?

Single-entry Bookkeeping

	A	B	C	D	E
1	**Assets**		YTD	Primo	
2	60	Louie	200	0	
3	40	Cash	0	200	
4	**Total assets**		211	200	
5					
6	**Date**		**Text**	**Amount**	
7	October 10		Louie	200,00	40 Cash
8	October 10		Louie	-200,00	60 Louie

Dewey wanted Louie to do his books, too, but since Dewey had neither revenue nor expenses, single-entry would do. In a fresh spreadsheet, make Dewey's books as shown here.

Since this is single-entry, there are no liabilities to balance the assets, and there are no retained earnings, either. The only thing that happened with Dewey's finances was that he borrowed $200 to Louie, so the single-entry bookkeeping fits in row 6, 7 and 8, as you can see.

29

The formula to calculate cell C2 is

$$=-\text{SUMIFS}(C:C,D:D,B2)$$

The formula to calculate cell C3 is

$$=-\text{SUMIFS}(C:C,D:D,B3)$$

The data validation on cells C7 and C8 is

Cell range	C7:C8
Criteria	List from range ◆ B2:B3

Notice that the bookkeeping for those accounts you choose to have is the same, whether you do single or double. With single entry, however, you can choose to have fewer accounts. Notice also that you can start with single, and then later change it to double, anytime you like.

Financial Ratios

	A	B	C
53	Note		
54		Return on assets	33%
55		Return on equity	51%
56		Gross margin	89%
57		Gearing	1.52

If you haven't already, make a sheet with your own bookkeeping or Louie's, so you have something to work with. In the bottom of that sheet, make this note.

Financial ratios are used to compare businesses and how well they're doing. They are calculated from the financial reports, like this, for the above four, using Louie's financial reports:

$$=C4/C10, \quad =C4/C13, \quad =C4/C2 \text{ and } =C10/C13$$

The ratios for Louie's business are not typical for real commercial enterprises. They are way too good. In a way, this is typical for a start-up. In the beginning the idea on which the business is built works well. Later, when things change, the business stays the same, and therefore the financial rations settle down, over time.

In Louie's case, since apples can only be picked a few months a year, he will have to find some other source of revenue, if he is to maintain his extraordinary financial ratios.

Perhaps the most important lesson in business is to manage capacity. Unless he finds another source of revenue, and because of the volatile nature of his supply of fresh apples, it would not be wise of Louie to buy an expensive printer, because he cannot realistically expect to sell enough apples to pay for such an increased administrative capacity, nor can he expect his elder family to keep funding his expansion.

Notice how business language sneaks itself in when one has to explain business matters with any degree of accuracy. The proverbial "earn before you spend" does not apply to the printer example above, because buying a printer doesn't affect earnings directly; it just moves some assets around in the balance sheet.

11 TROUBLESHOOTING

One of the techniques applied here is a very general one, sometimes called 'variation of parameters'. What the method amounts to, is that one changes bookkeeping records in a way that sheds light on the trouble. When applying variation of parameters, it must always be understood without saying, that the original records shall be restored once the troubleshooting is finished. This restoration of records is implicitly taken for granted and not explained or detailed in the Q&A section of this chapter.

Restore in Google Sheets can be done from `File/See revision history` (not the Chrome `File`, the Sheets `File`), and if the revisions listed are too old, newer ones are available by clicking `'Show more detailed revision'` at the bottom of the history list. In Excel, before you apply the methods detailed in this chapter, I strongly suggest you make a back-up copy of your workbook, just in case.

This troubleshooting guide is structured as a series of questions one could ask oneself, followed by a method for answering that question, often by deleting and reinserting bookkeeping records. One can delete and reinsert records in seconds by selecting the records in question and pressing the delete key followed by Ctrl-z. This works in both Google Sheets and Excel.

Questions & Answers

Question: The system does not work at all, why?

Answer: Delete all records except one or two simple transactions. You should now see assets, equity and liabilities balancing.

Question: The system as a whole does not add up bookkeeping records correctly, why?

Answer: Delete most records. Compare the remaining records with the financial report. You should now be able to spot report lines that do not add up.

Question: The sum in a specific reporting line is incorrect, why?

Answer: Copy the formula from a reporting line that adds up. If the culprit is a balance sheet report line, check that the formula includes the primo balance. If it is an asset account, check that the + and − signs are like it says in the balance sheet chapter.

Question: Assets and liabilities do not balance with equity, why?

Answer: Verify that the accounts used in the bookkeeping records are the same as those in the financial report. Check that the equity account is like it says in the bookkeeping chapter. Delete records successively until assets and liabilities balance equity, thus nailing down the records that cause the problem.

Question: The change in P&L cash balance does not agree with the Cash Flow, why?

Answer: Check that the Cash Flow report lines all together include all the balance sheet accounts except the earnings and the cash balance itself, as explained in the chapter about cash flow.

Question: Assets show up as negative numbers in the balance sheet, why?

Answer: Probably because they are really liabilities. Move them to that part of the financial report.

Question: Liabilities show up as negative numbers in the balance sheet, why?

Answer: Probably because they are really assets. Move them to that part of the financial report.

Question: The drop-down menu with the account list has disappeared from some field, why?

Answer: Probably because cut/paste was used on the field; it cuts the data validation too; use the delete key instead. This can be especially tricky when using a smartphone or a tablet, because the data validation is neither visible nor functional on those devices (at least it wasn't, at the time of writing).

Question: The system complains bitterly about a "circular reference" and sets certain fields to zero, why?

Answer: Probably because a formula was used in some bookkeeping record, a formula that references the financial reports. This is explained in the chapter about "Errors", under "Control Formulas".

Question: My 'Bank' report line does not match my bank-accounts balance, why?

Answer: Check for duplicate records. When you download this month's bank records from your Internet bank, there may be duplicate records.

Question: My 'Bank' report line still does not match my bank-accounts balance, why?

Answer: Check for canceled banking transfers. Some banks leave the canceled transfers in the download with a special marker that has no equivalent in this system.

Question: I need to check my bank-account records one-at-a-time, but my bank records are intermixed with non-bank records. How do I extract a pure bank-account ledger?

Answer: Specify Data filtering. This is explained in the chapter about "Journal and Ledger".

Question: I need to go through all records involving vendor so-and-so. How do I extract the relevant records?

Answer: Specify data filtering on the descriptive text of the bookkeeping records. The resulting drop-down list will display the various formats, which that vendors name has been entered with, for you to tick off.

Question: I have one account loaded with too many different kinds of cost, and I would like to split that up on several accounts. How do I do this smartly?

Answer: Use data filtering on the account number to pick out the relevant records. Select the records that need changing and use Find/Replace to change their accounts.

Question: My Excel system responds sluggishly yet does not appear defective. Why could that be?

Answer: The formulas use entire column array notation, e.g. D:D. This is smart because it places no hard limits on how many records and accounts the system can handle, but it has a performance drawback. If many empty records, say 10000, are added to a sheet, Excel will painstakingly work its way through them, thinking they might contain data. You can see whether this is the case by looking at the slider to the right of the sheet. If the slider is very small, it means the sheet is very big. Remove the empty records.

Question: My Google Sheets system appears buggy and unreliable, even though I've done everything right. Why could that be?

Answer: Probably because yours and Google's software have issues. Try switching to the Chrome browser. If you're already using Chrome, try temporarily switching to another platform (PC, Mac, iPad, Samsung…), to find out if the problem is with your platform or your spreadsheet.

Question: I have software issues with Google Sheets. Are there any tricks specific to this system, over and above those pertaining to general care and maintenance of software.

Answer: Spreadsheets are examples of cross-industry software deployed in, literally, billions of instances. Therefore you can be certain there exists some software combination that works. Seek out a software combination that works, instead of attempting to repair something that should work, but does not.

12 QUICK REFERENCE

	COLUMNS USED IN SHEET		
	Financial reports	**Bookkeeping**	**Notes**
A	Report line	Document number	Note header
B	Accounts	Date	Text
C	Formulas	Text	Formulas
D	Initial balance	Amount	
E		Left account	
F		Right account	

SPREADSHEET FUNCTIONS USED

x represents row number

=SUMIFS(D:D,E:E,Bx)-SUMIFS(D:D,F:F,Bx) *P&L and cash flow*

=Dx-SUMIFS(D:D,E:E,Bx)+SUMIFS(D:D,F:F,Bx) *for assets*

=Dx+SUMIFS(D:D,E:E,Bx)-SUMIFS(D:D,F:F,Bx) *for liabilities*

INDEX

accounting, 6
accounting policy, 25
accounting practices, 25
accounting relations, 27
accounts, 34, 35, 36
accounts numbering, 26
accounts organization, 26
America, 6
American, 6
array notation, 10, 36
asset, 34
assets, 4, 11, 12, 16, 20, 27, 29, 30, 34, 35, 37
back-door, 2
back-up, 33
balance sheet, 11, 34
balancing, 12, 34
bank account, 15, 19, 23, 24
bicycle, 1, 2
binder, 5
bookkeeping, 1, 3, 4, 5, 6, 7, 9, 10, 12, 15, 20, 23, 24, 25, 26, 27, 29, 30, 33, 34, 35, 36
business, 2, 4, 5, 7, 9, 13, 19, 20, 25, 30, 31
calculator, 28
cash, 1, 7, 11, 13, 14, 16, 20, 26, 34, 35, 37
cash flow, 4, 13, 16, 20, 34
cash flow from finance, 13
cash register, 5
cell, 6, 7, 9, 10, 12, 14, 17, 23, 28, 30
change, 10, 15, 25, 26, 27, 30, 34, 36
chart of accounts, 26
check, 34, 35
circular reference, 28
color, 12, 14
columns, 3
complicated, 4
computer, 3
conditional formatting, 12, 27
control formulas, 28, 35
cooking the books, 25
cost, 36
Ctrl-z, 33
data validation, 10, 14, 26, 30, 34, 35
date, 6, 7, 23
debt, 13, 25
decimal separator, 6, 9
deletion, 33
design, 3
Dewey, 1, 2, 5, 6, 11, 13, 16, 19, 25, 26, 29
Donald, 1, 2
double-entry, 3, 7
drop-down, 10, 14, 35, 36
drop-down menu, 35
earnings, 7, 13, 27, 29, 34
England, 6
equal sign, 27, 28
equipment, 11, 13, 28
equity, 7, 9, 11, 12, 14, 16, 20, 21, 26, 30, 34
errors, 12, 20, 25, 29
European, 6
Excel, 3, 33, 36
exercises, 29
expansion, 31
expenses, 6, 7, 9, 10, 16, 20, 25, 26, 28
explanatory notes, 15
extract, 35
filtering, 23, 35, 36
financial accounts, 13
financial ratios, 30
financial report, 3, 15, 19, 20, 34, 35
financial reports, 4, 20, 30, 35
find/replace, 36

formats, 6, 36
formula, 7, 9, 10, 12, 14, 17, 28, 30, 34, 35
formulas, 10, 17, 20, 36
fruit, 2
funding, 31
funky, 26
funnel, 23
getting started, 3
gifts, 2
Google Sheets, 3, 33, 36
grandma Duck, 2, 17
groups of companies, 19
Huey, 1, 2, 5, 6, 7, 11, 13, 16, 17, 19, 20, 21, 23, 25, 26, 28
illustration, 4
internet, 3, 35
journal, 23
journal & ledger, 23
lawn sale, 2
ledger, 23
left, 12, 20, 21, 28
lesson, 31
letters, 25
liabilities, 11, 12, 16, 20, 27, 29, 34, 37
liabilities & equity, 4, 11
loan, 2, 6, 23
lock, 2
Louie, 1, 2, 3, 5, 7, 9, 11, 13, 15, 17, 19, 20, 21, 23, 25, 26, 28, 29, 30, 31
Mac, 19, 36
machine, 1, 2
major and minor accounts, 26
mathematics, 27
matrix, 10
McDuck, 1, 15, 19, 20
merchant, 6
Microsoft, 3
misspelled, 10
money-box, 2, 5, 6, 7, 10, 15, 25
month-date format, 6

movements, 24
negative cash flow, 13
negative numbers, 34
net cash flow', 13
newspapers, 1, 28
notes, 17
Office, 3
operational accounts, 13
outdoor signs, 25
overlap, 20
P&L, 9, 34
payments, 7, 23
PC, 19, 36
performance, 36
plastic card, 23
presents, 1
primo, 11, 16, 20, 29
professional service, 43
profit & loss, 3, 4, 9, 16, 20
program, 3, 6, 10, 12, 23, 28
quick reference, 37
range, 10, 12, 14, 30
receipt, 5
records, 3, 4, 5, 7, 9, 10, 15, 20, 21, 23, 26, 28, 33, 34, 35, 36
red, 12
reference model, 4
reinsertion, 33
reject input, 27
reject input', 10
report lines, 4, 9, 10, 13, 14, 17, 34
restore, 33
retained earnings, 7
revenue, 7, 9, 15, 17, 29, 31
revision, 33
right, 20, 21, 28, 36
row, 7, 10, 12, 14, 23, 29, 37
rule, 12
salaries, 25
Scrooge, 1, 2, 3, 15, 17, 20
secret, 2, 17
sheet, 4, 11, 12, 14, 15, 26, 27, 30, 34, 36

simple, 4, 34
single-entry bookkeeping, 29
spreadsheet, 1, 3, 4, 6, 9, 10, 12, 19, 23, 24, 28, 29, 36
stakeholders, 20
start-up, 30
style, 26
sum, 4, 13, 27, 34
sumifs, 9, 10, 12, 14, 30, 37
system, 3, 4, 7, 10, 23, 26, 27, 34, 35, 36
tablet, 1, 2, 3, 5, 6, 15, 19, 25, 28

tax, 25
title, 4
transactions sheet, 35
troubleshooting, 33
two-level chart of accounts, 26
variation of parameters, 33
volatile, 31
wallet, 2, 15
warranty, 6
withdrawal, 7
workbook, 33
write-off, 28

ABOUT THE AUTHOR

Martin Mosfeldt is a Danish national and lives in Denmark on his country estate an hour west of Copenhagen. His CV and contact details are published separately on the World Wide Web. Some headlines:

- 1955 born in Denmark
- 1978 Master of Science in Engineering
- 1986 Advisory System Engineer, IBM
- 2001 Product Manager, Intel
- 2010 Master of Business Administration (Henley)

He has ten years of cross-industry management consulting experience obtained in small ICT oriented professional service firms. Since 2010 he has seen himself as a general businessperson with no affinity for any one particular industry over another.